MW00883347

Creative Confidence – The Missing Link in the Law of Attraction

How to tap into your Inner Creative Genius and get everything you want out of life.

"Each of us has within us an amazing idea, waiting to be birthed. It is our obligation to make the world a better place. The world needs more innovators and creators. If each of us took our one small idea.....we could in essence change the world. In the end, creativity is a choice - a choice we must make and teach our children to make." - Leslie Riopel

Leslie Riopel

Text copyright © 2014 Leslie D. Riopel. All rights reserved.

No part of this book may be reproduced or transmitted in any form or by any means, graphic, electronic, or mechanical, including photocopying, recording, taping, or by any information storage retrieval system, without the permission, in writing, of the publisher.

Disclaimer Notice:

Please note the information contained within this document is for educational purposes only.

Every attempt has been made to provide accurate, up-to-date, and reliable complete information. No warranties of any kind are expressed or implied. Readers acknowledge that the author is not engaging in rendering legal, financial, or professional advice.

By reading any document, the reader agrees that under no circumstances are we responsible for any losses, direct or indirect, which are incurred as a result of use of the information contained within this document, including but not limited to errors, omissions, or inaccuracies.

Table of Contents

Creative Confidence

Chapter One – What is Creative Confidence?

"Creativity does not come from you as much as it flows through you." - Leslie Riopel

What exactly is creative confidence? Creative confidence is really all about realizing the fact that each of us is gifted with virtually an unlimited potential for learning and creativity.The fact of the matter is that every single one of us is born as a genius! It's only when we are told what to do and how to do it that we begin to lose this natural creativity.

The human brain is amazing in the fact that it has approximately 86 billion neurons! For a long time neuroscientists believed that there were close to 100 billion neurons in the human brain, however, no peer-reviewed journal or scientific paper has really supported that particular number. A more recent study done in 2009 showed that the number was actually closer to 86 billion, rather than 100 billion.

Either way, that's a lot of neurons! The truth is the brain's neuronal density isn't uniform at all and it is hard to estimate the number of neurons in each of the brain's regions. What is clear from these numbers is the human brain is an amazingly complex organ. Scientists can probably agree that we have barely tapped into its potential.

Research shows us that in a series of I.Q. tests given to children 2 – 4 years of age that approximately 95% of them were found to be highly creative. Test results showed that children of this age hadcurious, questioning minds with anincredible ability for abstract thinking.

However, when these same children were tested again at the age of 7, only a small number of them, around 5% demonstrated this same level of creativity. In light of this we have to ask ourselves what happened? What happened is that children were "taught to conform" which is a shame. They lost their childlike enthusiasm and pension for creative thought.

While I'm certainly not saying that our educational system is to blame, what I am saying is that all of us are born with this natural ability and over time we tend to lose it. Since our brains have over 86 billion neurons, it makes sense that perhaps we still have the ability to tap into this creative thought process even as adults. In my opinion, creativity is not something you either have or don't have - it's more like a muscle you have to continually use.

As kids we learn to color inside the lines, sit in neat little rows and do what we are supposed to do. We learn to follow directions and to follow the leader. While that may be a great trait for conformity, it does little in support of creativity and innovation. The sad truth is that creativity, imagination and innovation is often discouraged. We are told how to think and how to feel and what to do. Over time, we lose that amazing spontaneity as we learn to suppress ideas and insights that are unusual or different.

The good news is that creativity is one of those skills that lie latent until you are ready to use it. The ability to be creative never really diminishes. Creativity is your birthright, and a fundamental part of your nature and you can tap into it at any time, no matter how long it has been since you have really used it.

Everything in life requires creative thought because life is one big problem solving opportunity. While those in the art, design and engineering fields may use creative thinking as part of their jobs, that doesn't mean that the rest of us don't need it. Most of us are challenged with a problem every day whether it's how to make our money stretch or how to find more time to spend with our family.

Creative confidence may be better defined as having both the courage and freedom to fail and take creative risks. When you look at someone like Thomas Edison, you see that he had a very different idea of "failure" than others. He believed that ALL ideas had value and he looked at nothing as a failure, as we see in the quote below.

"I have not failed 1,000 times. I have successfully discovered 1,000 ways to NOT make a light bulb." - Thomas Edison

When creating the light bulb, Thomas Edison "failed" multiple times, but he didn't really look at those failed attempts as failures, he looked at them as stepping-stones to his success. He believed that his mistakes were meant to teach him something and he used those failed attempts to make the necessary adjustments and changes along the way. The result was the innovation of the light bulb so I think we can all agree his failures were a huge success.

Everything in life requires creativity....whether you realize it or not. The need to be creative is always upon you, whether it is thinking up a creative solution to a problem or creating a masterpiece out of clay.

Each of us can connect with our creative side and each of us can learn the dynamics of our creative mind and how to invite its insights and perspectives into our daily lives. This often-untapped power of our mind can transform our lives in unimagined ways, from solving our most mundane needs to realizing our highest aspirations.

We often look to outside sources for creativity and inspiration but the real truth is that all creativity comes from within and each of is capable of tapping into this amazing life changing power.

"Most men lead lives of quiet desperation and go to the grave with the song still in them."— Henry David Thoreau, Civil Disobedience and Other Essays

This quote by Henry David Thoreau, describes many of us. If you are living a life far below your own potential for joy, accomplishment or success, you are in a sense a prisoner of your own doing. While this book is called "Creative Confidence", what it's really about is learning how to tap into that incredible power that lies within. It's about tapping into your own inner genius and learning how to live life joyfully, and with freedom, power and a sense of purpose.

Each of us has a creative soul inside of us; some of us have learned how to tap into this part of ourselves, while others have not. There are some who tend to be more naturally creative, but I would argue that creativity is not something you either have or don't have. It is a skill everyone has access to, and whether you are right brained or left brained does not really matter.

The truth is that the world needs more creative and innovative souls. It doesn't matter if you are an accountant or a world famous designer, because every job or station in life needs those who are innovative and creative. Without innovation, the world remains stagnate.

I believe each of us has an endless capacity for knowledge. Change and innovation are our birthright. If we are not growing, and learning and changing we are in essence dying. Change is inventible; we can either embrace it or defy it.

"If you hear a voice within you say, 'You can not paint,' then by all means paint, and that voice will be silenced" – Vincent Van Gogh

This book focuses on the common man – not on those within the corporate industry, although anyone can benefit from using these techniques. There are plenty of great books about corporate innovation, and this book is not meant to compete with those.

The focus of this book is to help people realize that flexing that creative muscle can help them in every area of life, from their relationships, to their job to their finances. We all need to be creative in order to solve problems.

"Problems cannot be solved with the same mind set that created them." – Albert Einstein

Just like Albert Einstein said in the famous quote above that our problems couldn't often be solved in the same mindset that created them, the problems of life cannot often be solved in a logical or concrete manner.

Thinking outside the box can help you expand your creativity. Most of us grew up with the idea that our intelligence was firmly set at a specific number, thanks to the IQ test. I would argue that the IQ test does not matter as much as your ability to want to learn and improve.

The idea of creative confidence is integral to your sense of peace and happiness in the world. When you have the tools you need to tap into this creative ability, there is no problem you cannot solve. While the business world certainly needs creative thinkers, I would propose that the world itself needs creative thinkers much more. We all have an ability to change the world – and creative confidence can help us do just that.

"Never underestimate the power of a small group of committed people to change the world, in fact, it the only thing that ever has. – Margaret Mead

This book is all about tapping into your God given right to creative thought. You have all the gifts you need right inside your amazing mind and brain. You create your own reality – all within your thoughts. You can use this power to make your life more satisfying and gratifying.

When you take small steps toward your goals, you can begin to think and dream in unlimited ways. I promise you this book will both motivate and inspire you to change your thinking and it will do so in a clear and concise manner.I have spent over 24 years in the Corporate World as an Interior Designer and

Facilities Manager, so I know a thing or two about the creative thought process.

As a Clinical Hypnotherapist and Freelance Writer with a master's degree in Psychology Health and Wellness, I have seen the effects that creativity can have on one's life. I have seen it in my students as well as with my clients. Those who believe in the power of their own creative thought tend to do much better in life.

So if you're ready, I would like to take you on a journey that quite possibly could change your life. I know it changed mine. If you will join me on this journey, I will you show the way to transform your life all using the power of your own innate creativity.

Chapter Two – Fixed Versus Growth Mindset

"Some of the most innovative and successful people in the world are also the most creative." Leslie Riopel

Each of us has been gifted with a practicallyunlimited potential for learning and creativity. Much of what we know about the capabilities of the human brain has been learned in the last twenty years or so.

Our schools, Universities and our businesses are just now beginning to apply some of this emerging knowledge. Many of us grew up with the concept of knowledge and intelligence that was based solely on the lonely IQ Test. What this test assumes is that intelligenceis something that is fixed….and that once you are labeled as a number, you become that number forever more.

As an Interior Designer and freelance writer, my source of creativity and intelligence lies within me and every day I make a choice to learn, and grow and change. I don't hold much stock in the

IQ number other than a point of reference.

My work is dependent upon this ability to be creative and to motivate and inspire people, and without it, I would be lost.

Stretching Your Creativity

There are many things you can do to stretch your creativity and imagination, and we will investigate some of them in this book. While this is not an exact science, it can help you to start thinking differently.

The Alternative Uses test developed by J.P. Guilford in 1967 is a great creativity stretcher. The test uses the idea of everyday objects challenging you to find as many possible uses for everyday objects, other than their intended use.

Let's look at something like a coffee mug. Try this now. Give yourself 2 minutes to come up with as many different uses for a coffee mug that you can think of. Don't cheat. Go ahead and do this now. We will review the possible answers at the end of the chapter.

Fixed Versus Growth Mindset

Psychologists speak in terms of a fixed versus a growth mindset. Those with a fixed mindset believe that their talent or intelligence are "fixed" traits. Those with a growth mindset on the other hand believe that their basic abilities can be developed through hard work and dedication.

Carol Dweck, a world-renowned psychologist spent decades researching the idea of achievement and success and the idea of the mindset, and your mindset can explain a lot about how you view your life

Those with a fixed mindset may not see that they have this potential for change,so they may not take further steps to develop it. The growth mindset looks at talent and intelligence as just a starting point, this point of view creates a love of learning and a great sense of resilience. Those who are successful, tend to have a growth mindset, and they never stop learning and growing and changing.

If you can learn to switch your mindset from a fixed one, which is extremely limiting, to a growth one, which is virtually unlimited, everything you touch will be successful. Having this kind of mindset can enhance every area of your life, from your personal relationships to your career.

Take a moment to stop and ask yourself what kind of mindset you tend to have - and be honest with yourself. It's OK if you think your mindset tends to be more fixed, because identifying the problem is the first step towards improvement.

Fixed Mindset Traits

- Intelligence is fixed and static
- Leads to the idea that you need to appear smart
- You tend to avoid challenges
- You give up easily
- You see effort as fruitless or worse
- You feel threatened by the success of others
- You may plateau early in life and achieve less than your full potential

Growth Mindset Traits

- Intelligence can be developed
- You have a desire to learn and grow
- You embrace change
- You persist in the face of setbacks
- You see effort as the path to self-mastery
- You find lessons and inspiration in others success
- You reach higher and higher levels of achievement because of this viewpoint

When you can learn to tap into your own innate creativity and intelligence, there is no limit to what you can achieve. The idea of creativity is not a one-size fits all kind of thing - there are many ways to use your creativity, from your finances to your personal life. Let's look at the possible answers now to the alternative uses of a coffee mug.

Alternative uses for a coffee mug

1. Pencil cup
2. Make-up brush holder
3. Spare change container
4. Make them into candle holders

5. Make "one cup cookies "or "mug cakes"
6. Create gifts out of them by filling them with chocolate or bath beads
7. Use it to hold sweetener packets
8. Use in a craft room for buttons, scissors, paintbrushes etc.
9. Small tool holder like screwdrivers
10. Bust them up and use them for a mosaic art piece
11. Coupon organizer
12. Easter egg dye holder for different colors
13. Men's shaving item holder
14. Scoop for pet food
15. Herb garden holder
16. Jewelry holder for small items
17. Ponytail and hair item holder
18. Seedling starters
19. Workbench holder for small screws and washers
20. Use as a ladle or measuring cup
21. Repurpose into an art piece like a lamp
22. Silverware holder
23. Dinner side dish container for beans or applesauce
24. Tooth brush holder
25. Toothpaste holder

26. Donate to a shelter or take them to work
27. Candy dishes

Chapter Three: The Law of InfinitePossibilities

"Some look at things that are, and ask why. I dream of things that never were and ask why not? - Bernard Shaw.

This quote by Bernard Shaw encapsulates the spirit I want to convey when it comes to creativity. There are an infinite number of possible outcomes for anything you do. The trouble is we often get lost in our limited thought process to the point that it's hard to think of creative possibilities.

Wayne Dyer, an internationally renowned author and inspirational speaker said it quite nicely when he said: "If you change the way you look at things, the things you look at change." The concept of infinite possibilities can really change your viewpoint. This law is about changing your perspective and expanding your mind, and asking yourself "What if this weren't true?"

Many of us have preconceived ideas about how we can solve a problem. Our conscious mind is very limited because it can only hold a small amount of information at any given time. Albert Einstein knew this, which is why he is famous for his quote where he said problems couldn't often be solved in the same frame of mind they were created in.

We don't often take advantage of the limitless thinking our more creative subconscious mind offers us, because most of the time we beat our heads against the wall time after time again trying to come up creative and unique solutions to our problems using our somewhat limited conscious mind.

When was the last time you had a great idea sitting at your desk at work? How about when you were trying to come up with a creative solution to solve a problem? If you could open up your mind to explore the infinite possibilities that may exist, you open yourself up to a multitude of new solutions. Think about this for a minute. What are some of the beliefs that you hold true? Think about why you believe these to be true? What if they were not true? What if...........Imagine the possibilities!

We usually get our best ideas when we are not thinking about the problem. This is exactly why you tend to get great ideas in the shower or when you are out driving around in the car. The best thing to do if you feel stuck is to walk away and go do something else for a while. Those who think more creatively know that their creativity works better if they give their mind something to chew on while they're doing something else.

You can actually program your mind and ask it to come up with creative solutions, and it's easier than you might think.

Subconscious Versus Conscious Mind

You actually go in and out of different states of mind on a regular basis every time you miss an exit on the highway or get lost in thought. Anything that causes your mind to wander stimulates your imagination and creates a suggestible state; all of which can be used to help you boost your creativity and imagination.

Your subconscious mind is like a preprogrammed car on autopilot. It will take the familiar road, whether you want to go there or not. It has no ability to steer itself in a new direction, because it follows whatever is programmed into it over time.

The conscious mind is the tip of the iceberg per se because it can only retain a small amount of information at any one time. The unconscious or subconscious mind is where most of your information is stored and that information guides your life. All of those little thoughts you think about and repeat day and in and day out rule your life. Your thoughts become things so it pays to think positive. Many of us dwell on those things that aggravate or annoy us. If we continually tell ourselves that we are unsuccessful, lazy or unmotivated to eat healthy, then that is what continues to manifest in our life.

Your life is a self-fulfilling prophecy because whatever you continually dwell on or think about comes about. Sigmund Freud, although he certainly did not invent the idea of the conscious versus the unconscious mind, did make it very popular and better known. Freud compared the mind to an iceberg in the fact that the conscious mind only represents the very tip of the iceberg. The unconscious mind or that which lies below our conscious thoughts stores a much more vast amount of information. He believed that while we are fully aware of what is going on in the conscious mind, most of us have little to no idea of what kind of information is stored in the unconscious mind.

According to Albert Einstein, imagination is more important than knowledge. The subconscious mind does not know the difference between reality and imagination, so when you replay a scenario in your mind, the mind takes it as fact. Visualization and tools like meditation are very powerful tools and you can literally use them to change your life. When you can learn to use your imagination you begin to convert thoughts and feelings into mental images. Those mental images are perceived as reality by your subconscious mind, so eventually your mind brings those mental images into your world.

When you begin to see things in your mind's eye you bring those things into your reality. When you can feel it, see it, taste it and experience it in your mind, you send a powerful signal out to the world through your energy. In other words, your thoughts really do become things - there is simply a time delay in which they manifest.

Autonomic Nervous System

In order to further understand how your mind works, you must first understand how the nervous system works. There are two distinct nervous systems in the human body– the Central Nervous System and the Autonomic Nervous System. The Central Nervous System or CNS is the processing center of the nervous system and it utilizes the brain and the spinal cord.

The Autonomic Nervous System or ANS as we will call it regulates the functions of your internal organs such as your heart, stomach and intensities. The ANS has two divisions, the sympathetic and the parasympathetic nervous system.

The sympathetic nervous system or SNS controls your ability to respond to emergencies – in other words it is your fight or flight syndrome. The SNS controls your heart rate, your respiration and even your blood pressure. This system also releases adrenaline to give you energy if you need it during an emergency. The SNS can also come into play when you are nervous or anxious.

The parasympathetic nervous system or PNS creates the opposite response. It slows down the rate of the heart, the blood pressure and even the respiration. The PNS restores the body to a state of peace of calm so that the body can conserve energy.

These two systems cannot operate at the same time. When you meditate or relax deeplyyou can activate the PNS in order to help your mind and body to relax. When you are able to relax deeply, you are able to tap into your subconscious mind, where changes are more easily made.

Using your imagination, you can create powerful visualizations that reflect the life you want to be living.

Your mind also goes in and out of different brainwave frequencies on a regular basis. The Alpha brainwave state is the state most often accessed during relaxation or meditation.

The Beta brainwave state is the dominant state of mind most of us are in during the course of our day and the Beta brainwave state typically corresponds to a frequency level of about 12 to 40 Hz.

The Alpha brainwave state operates at about 8 to 12 Hz, which is a little slower than the Beta state. The Alpha brainwave state is often associated with an extremely relaxed state of mind and this relaxed state of mind is very conducive to imagination or creativity. When you contemplate or problem solve, you are also accessing the Alpha brainwave state.

The Theta brainwave state is even slower than Alpha and it operates at around 4 to 8 Hz. Theta is a very deep state of relaxation or light sleep and it is the state of mind most often accessed during meditation or even hypnosis. One of the deepest and slowest brainwave states is Delta and it occurs around 0 to 4

Hz. Delta brainwave states typically occur in very deep sleep, and this level of mind is not typically accessed during meditation.

Accessing the Alpha brainwave state can help you tap into that innate creativity that can give you the creative confidence you need in order to supercharge your life.

The mind processes things differently depending on whether or not you sense things in a visual, auditory manner or a kinesthetic manner. This is also known as VAK. Each of us sees things from a different perspective. If you are an auditory person you most likely use your sense of hearing rather than your sense of sight. In other words, you may relax more while listening to soothing music as opposed to thinking of a beautiful beach.

If you process information in a visual manner, you probably love the idea of a beautiful serene beach, because you can actually see the beach in your mind's eye. If you are more of a kinesthetic processor you might like to imagine yourself touching the sand or imagine walking with your feet immersed in the water.

Visualization is an incredibly powerful tool that can help you focus and directs your imagination. It might also be called mental imagery or even guided imagery. Research has shown that stimulating the brain through imagery may have a direct effect on both the endocrine system and the nervous system, leading to changes in immune system function. The only requirement to making visualization or guided imagery work for you is the use of your imagination.

Guided Imagery has even been used in hospitals to help patients cope better with illnesses. If you can use your imagination to help yourself heal, you can certainly use it to tap into your imagination and creative ability.

Guided imagery and visualization are relaxation techniques that can ease stress and promote a sense of peace and tranquility. It can be used by anyone, including young children up through the elderly, because it is a process that allows you to tap into your imagination.

Endorphins are your body's feel good chemicals and they are produced naturally by a wide range of activities including running, meditating and practices like Guided Imagery. Guided Imagery can even help reduce pain and stimulate healing by releasing powerful pain reducing endorphins in the brain.

MRI's have shown that when people think of beautiful places, they actually trigger the parts of the brain that register various senses helping to elicit healing. Other ways to release endorphins are by laughing, utilizing your imagination and/or daydreaming or by simply meditating or breathing deeply.

Guided Imagery and Visualization can be used for many things including but not limited to:

- Reduce and manage pain symptoms.
- Reduce stress and anxiety.
- Improve mental and emotional health.
- Help solve problems and boost creative confidence.
- Reduce insomnia.

- Help you prepare for surgery or medical procedures.
- Speed up healing.
- Help with anger.
- Help with weight loss.
- Help overcome addictions.
- Help with behavior modification.
- Post Traumatic Stress.

Using these tools you can counteract worry, negative experiences, and uncomfortable symptoms and think yourself well!

Chapter Four: Day DreamingAnd TheCreative Thought Library

Wouldn't you love to create a place where you could go to boost your imagination and your creative confidence? The truth is you can, by looking inside your own very creative mind. Note that I am assuming you are already creative. If you have been reading this book thinking that you are not a creative person, this exercise will convince you otherwise. While there are certainly many books you could read on the subject of creativity or even creative confidence, there aren't that many that actually give you the tools you need to start working on building your own creative confidence.

Creating a creative thought library is a lot of fun because it allows you to expand your mind. This tool is similar to meditation and guided imagery, but at the same time very different. While visualization and guided imagery tend to be focused on very specific things, the creative thought library is a place where you can go in your mind to tap into a sort of universal consciousness.

There is a theory that nothing new is ever created, because everything has been done before. If you have a problem, chances are someone else in the past has also had that problem at one time or another.

If you are a bit intimated about using your imagination to boost your creativity, all you really need to do is think back to how you entertained yourself when you were a child. As children, it's easy for us to get lost in daydreams and fantasies. The problem is that way of thinking is quickly discouraged. In school, you were usually reprimanded if you got lost in thought or lost in your playful daydreams.

The world is built by dreamers so if you want to start thinking more creatively, you have to learn how to imagine and daydream all over again.

It's a shame that daydreaming gets a bad rap in our modern day society. If you haven't daydreamed in a while, you might be surprised at the advantages it has. A new study reported in the journal of Psychological Science suggests that daydreaming boosts creativity. Researchers from the University of California in Santa Barbara also discovered an association between daydreaming and creative problem solving.

The study had participants try and come up with as many weird ways to use an object as they could. Note the similarities between this study and the Alternative Uses test first developed by J.P. Guilford.

The study participants did one out of these four things before starting the experiment:

1. Performed a demanding task where their attention was completely absorbed in the task;
2. Performed an undemanding task;
3. Took a 12-minute break;
4. Skipped the 12-minute break and moved right into the exercise.

What the researchers found was that the only group that did better when performing the test the second time around were the participants who completed the "undemanding task" first. Researchers speculated that since the participants reported that they daydreamed while completing the undemanding task that their mind wandering most likely contributed to their higher scores on the creative challenge.

What this data suggests, according to the researchers, is that engaging in simple external tasks allows the mind to wander, which may facilitate creative problem solving. Another study done in the same journal also showed that daydreaming could also be good for your working memory. Your working memory enables you to think about multiple things at once, and it may be linked to your intelligence. Researchers from the Max Planck Institute for Human Cognitive and Brain Science found that those whose minds wandered during a simple task were also the ones with greater working memory.

While daydreaming is powerful, using your imagination is even more powerful.

Albert Einstein used his powerful imagination to develop the theory of relativity. He imagined himself riding on a beam of light in his now infamous "thought experiment." Because of this ability to use his imagination and to theorize and experiment in his mind, he developed the theory of relativity.

As children we are taught to color within the lines, follow the rules, and be good little boys and girls. Albert Einstein certainly didn't follow the rules and look where that got him!

As children, we are of course naturally creative. We love to play make-believe and use our imagination. Little by little, this talent is squelched as we learn to follow the rules and color within the lines.

Because of this, we develop a fear of failure and we learn over time that it is better to stay within the guidelines than to stray off course. Those that choose the path of creativity in life might choose to be artists or designers, but the reality is that each of us has that creative spark inside us. Those who aspire to be creative souls are often poked fun at for their crazy non-standard ways. The typically "abnormal" behavior of the creative person may be described as careless, maladjusted or even wacky. When we think of someone creative, our minds often drift to a Bohemian type of artist dressed in colorful clothing or someone living a life out of alignment with the rest of us.

Experts estimate that many of us spend up to one-half of our waking hours daydreaming. That figure may shock you, but it makes sense if you think about it. Think about all those times when you are standing in line at the grocery store or driving around in your car, and chances are you will realize that your mind was most likely wandering.

According to the Dartmouth Undergraduate Journal of Science, daydreaming is not only a normal part of our cognitive functioning and processes, it can also be a very beneficial process as well.

The real truth is that daydreaming has many rewards. When you daydream, you give your mind a workout. The area of your brain accountable for daydreaming has been called the default network. This area of your brain becomes much more active when the stimulus level around you diminishes. Your mind is very active during a daydream.

According to Marcus Raichle, a neurologist at Washington University, "When you don't use a muscle, that muscle isn't doing much, but when your brain is supposedly doing nothing and daydreaming, it's doing a tremendous amount of work. Scientists call it a resting state, but the brain is not at rest at all."

Many of us are under the misconception that daydreaming is a wasteful usage of our time, but the reality is that daydreaming can actually help you live your life in a healthier manner.

An article by a Christine Dell'Amore of National Geographic suggests that daydreaming can make you more creative since the thoughts that occur during a daydreaming episode tend to rotate through different parts of the brain - accessing information that may have been dormant. Daydreaming may even help you make an association between those little bits of information you have never considered in a particular way before. This process helps fuel creativity and may also help offer you solutions to problems that you had not yet considered, according to Eugenio M.

Rothe, a psychiatrist at Florida International University.

According to Christina Frank of WebMD, daydreaming has many benefits including:

- Daydreaming can help you relax;
- Daydreaming can help you manage conflict;
- Daydreaming can help you better maintain relationships;
- Daydreaming can help boost your productivity.

Just like meditation, daydreaming allows you to relax because it allows your mind to take a break from reality. Both meditation and daydreaming help you release tension leaving you more refreshed.

According to research, daydreaming can help you manage conflict better because you can review the problem in your mind and then respond to the conflict differently in reality. Daydreaming can also help you in your personal relationships because you may tend to think about someone when you're apart, which can help maintain the relationship on a psychological level.

According to James Honeycutt, PhD, author of Imagined Interactions, daydreaming allows you to imagine sharing news with your loved one, along with your successes and failures, which may help nurture the relationship in the long run.

Daydreaming can also boost your productivity according to Cari Noga, a freelance writer in Traverse City, Michigan who states that a few minutes of daydreaming can help make you more productive in the long run.

When you daydream, nothing is impossible. When you daydream you tend to dream big, and you end up working harder to make your dream a reality. Olympic athletes use visualization, which is really just another form of daydreaming, to help their performance in the same way that actual physical practice does.

It is apparent that daydreaming is normal and it can have many have benefits for your mental health. While it may not provide relief for those suffering from a severe mental illness, it can be a great tool for those looking to boost their creativity.

Give Yourself Permission to Dream - The "What If" Exercise and More

A great way to get your creative juices flowing is to play the "what if" game. These two words help free your imagination so you can start thinking differently. The best way to play this game is to start by thinking of something that couldn't or wouldn't happen in this world. Try this simple exercise now.

What if you could jump into a parallel universe any time you wanted? How would that change your life?

- Would you stay in your current life or immediately jump to a new one?
- If you decided to jump to a new one, how would it be different?
- What does it look like in this parallel universe?

- Are there people you know here, or do you have a whole new set of friends in your life?
- Is your family the same or are they different?
- Do you have a new love relationship in this new universe, or is it the same?
- What kind of a job or career do you have in this new universe?
- How are you different in this world?
- What kind of a house do you live in?
- What kind of a town do you live in?

Let's try another one now.

What if you had made different decisions in your life or had chosen a different path somewhere along the way?

- How would your life be different?
- What kind of new choices have you made?
- If you came to a fork in the road, and were suddenly given the opportunity to take a new road, how would your life be different?

- How has this new choice affected your life?
- Do you have a new career?
- Do you have a different love relationship?
- What else is different in your life?
- How has this new choice affected your level of happiness?

These kinds of mind exercises are fun to do, because they help you stretch your imagination. The more you think this way, the easier it is to think outside of the box.

Creating a Creative Thought Library

When you daydream, your mind drifts into the alpha brainwave state. When your mind is in alpha, your creative mind and imagination take over and your subconscious mind comes to the forefront. Your brilliant subconscious mind doesn't distinguish between reality and imagination, as we have seen, so whatever you think or dream about, is real in your mind.

In this more relaxed state of mind your subconscious mind is more easily able to to resolve problems that your conscious mind might have difficulty resolving. When you daydream you clear your mind, which helps give you new inspiration and energy. Doing this allows your brain to create new neural networks which helps you think and dream in unlimited ways. These new neural networks are the source of both inspiration and innovation.

Daniel J. Levitin, the author ofThe Organized Mind: Thinking Straight in the Age of Information Overload quotes:

"Daydreaming leads to creativity, and creative activities teach us agency, (which is) the ability to change the world, to mold it to our liking, to have a positive effect on our environment."

There is probably no better example of the power of daydreaming than the Google headquarters office in Zurich, Switzerland. Google has taken the idea of fun and daydreaming right into the workplace - and no one would question their profitability!

The building was designed partly by their 300 engineers who work there and it is the epitome of the crazy office. They have meeting roomsthat look like chalets and igloos, and even fireman poles for access between floors. The cafeteria has a slide so that people can get there as quickly as possible.

The message this sends to its employees is that they are free to be creative and innovative and the environment certainly supports this. Creativity is encouraged and highly valued. The space has bright vibrant colors and a crazy feel making employees feel much more comfortable.

Google's staff rooms are designed much like playrooms with crazy shapes and bursts of color. Whiteboards and beanbag chairs encourage creative thinking and brainstorming and individual workplaces encourage the flow of creative thought. One thing is for sure, Google certainly knows that creativity is not a stagnate process and creativity cannot often be found in a boring office setup or a 5x7 cube.

When employees are allowed to relax and let their hair down, their productivity levels most likely skyrocket. In today's world with the invention of laptops and mobile devices, employees can essentially work anywhere and people are no longer tied to a desk.

What Does Your Creative Thought Library Look Like?

This exercise is the epitome of creative thinking. When you create a space in your mind where you can go relax and let your hair down, you allow your creativity to flourish. Think about what kind of place you would go to if you wanted to push the limits of your creativity? This creative thought library has everything you need to tap into your creativity.

The point of this exercise is to have fun and to allow your mind to wander. This place is like a mental problem solving lab of sorts or a daydreaming lab. Now think about what kind of room you would be in that was designed exactly to your liking. Imagine somewhere creative yet peaceful. What kind of place do you dream about? Everyone is different, so your creativity lab might be clean and open or it may be more casual or cluttered, whatever works for you.

This kind of place is somewhere where you can go to explore the limits of your creativity and imagination. It is the ideal place to incubate your goals and rethink your life dreams.

Suggestions for locations for your creative thought library

- Mountain top temple
- Cozy Beach House
- Tree house in the forest
- Japanese Tea House in an exotic garden
- Palatial castle
- Deep inside a cave
- A building deep underneath the sea
- Somewhere in the Amazon Rainforest
- A desert hideaway
- A country estate
- Glass temple in the sky

- Religious temple or monastery
- A Tropical Garden
- A cafe in Paris
- Chalet in the Swiss Alps

Leslie Riopel

There are no boundaries so use your creativity and imagination to push the limits of your mind. Think of somewhere you would feel safe and secure. This might be different every time you do this exercise. I like to imagine myself sitting on a wooden deck of a tiny little Japanese Tea House built just for me. In my Tea House I have everything I need. It is located near a small stream where I can listen to the water and there are also wind chimes on the deck.

When I meditate and reflect, I often take myself here in my mind. I also like to listen to environmental sounds like birds singing and water flowing so that I can take myself their even easier.

Now in your mind, start imagining what kinds of things you have in this place. If you have imagined yourself outdoors, go inside and start creating an environment or room that fosters your creativity. Fill the room with creative tools like:

- Whiteboards and markers
- Easel pads
- Comfortable chairs
- Paint brushes
- All the books you need
- Corkboard wall for notes
- Computer
- Writing surfaces
- Flow chart wall
- Anything else you can imagine.....

You might also consider creating a space in the room with two chairs seated in front of a window. In this space you can bring in a creative advisor or someone who can help you generate ideas. You can imagine yourself sitting with Albert Einstein or even Thomas Edison or Steve Jobs, anyone you think or dream of. Bring in anyone you want to help you tap into your creativity and imagination.

This sanctuary is your Creative Thought Library and in it you'll find all the tools you need to solve problems, refresh your energy, incubate ideas, receive guidance and nurture your sense of self. Anything you can imagine and want to imagine can go into this library.

Now add anything else you think you need like a large viewing screen or theatre in the round; a beautiful garden with water or pools, a terrace or deck, or even a magical doorway that leads to other places in this library.

When you let your imagination run free and you start to have fun with your creativity, there is no limit to what kind of solutions you might come up with.

Think of this place like a holographic structure that becomes more real and more vivid each time you visit it. You will eventually get to the point where you can enter this daydreaming mode in a matter of minutes, every time you close your eyes and allow your mind to wander. This place is a very powerful place for healing, problem solving, future planning and even manifesting.

In part two of of the book we will dive deeper into this concept, helping you use your creative mind to manifest anything in life you want, need or desire.

Chapter Five: Unlocking Your Body's Energy Meridians

There are of course many tools you can use to unlock your natural creativity. No book on creative confidence would be complete without enlightening you on the idea of the energy meridians in your body.

Based on the concept of Chinese medicine and acupressure, you have access to an invisible network of energy within your own body. These energetic pathways create your life force energy or chi and accessing them by techniques such as acupressure or EFT, Emotional Freedom Technique, can help you release stuck or stagnate energy.

When you have a creative block or you feel like you are stuck in some part of your life, working with your network of energy can work miracles, if you use it as a complementary tool.

Gary Craig first developed EFT and he has taught the technique to hundreds of thousands of people. By tapping the energy meridians in your body and repeating affirming statements, you can overcome issues you have been struggling with in a matter of a few sessions.

EFT is a process where you tap with your fingertips on specific acupressure points while concentrating on a problem or issue. It allows you to transform uncomfortable feelings like guilt, anger or even fear. Our emotions can have a powerful impact on our mind, body and spirit, but sometimes our emotions can hold us back.

The creative process is something you can "tap into" and once you access it, it will flow freely through you. Creativity can help you boost your human potential, and it can help you supercharge your life. Each of us has a creative and innovative side to us; some people have just never discovered theirs.

Whether you want to write a book or solve the problems of the world, EFT provides you with one more tool that can help you tap into your own creative thought process. While this book is not specifically about EFT, you can use these simple techniques the next time you are stuck for an idea.

EFT is really just a form of psychological acupressure, based on the same energy meridians used in acupuncture to treat both physical and emotional ailments. Instead of using needles, you can use your fingertips. When you tap with the fingertips you release a sort of kinetic energy onto very specific energy meridians while you think about your specific problem. While you are tapping you also say affirmations.

The combination of tapping the energy meridians and repeating affirmations works in a sense by clearing the "short-circuit" - or emotional block from your body's bioenergy system. EFT restores your mind and body's balance, which is essential for good emotional and physical health.

Some people may equate EFT with the electromagnetic energy that flows through the body, like magnetic healing. Magnets are becoming much more accepted in terms of healing disease and they are gaining more popularity every day. Electromagnetic therapy is an up and coming science and one that has recently gotten a lot more attention. The truth is that not many people fully understand exactly how the earth's magnetic field really affects human health. There are many theories but not a lot of consensus.

Typically EFT is done with the index and middle finger using one hand; it doesn't matter if you use the left or right hand. Many of the tapping or acupressure points are located on either side of the body, so you can use whatever hand or side you like.

The tapping points shown below form the basis of EFT. Start at the top of the head, by tapping the center of your skull. Move down to the eyebrow by tapping just above and to one side of the nose, at the beginning of the eyebrow as shown.

The next point is the side of the eye, on the bone near the outside corner. Tap under the eye next on the bone about one inch below the pupil. The next point is under the nose, on that small area between the bottom of the nose and the top of your upper lip.

Move next to the chin and tap midway between the point on your chin and the bottom of your lower lip. The collarbone is next, just tap at the junction where your breastbone or sternum, collarbone and first rib meet. The last two points are under the arm, even with the nipple and the wrists.

Now I know this may sound very strange, but using your own energy to free your innate creativity, may just be the best thing you'll ever try! You can also use EFT to overcome other challenges like addictions or weight loss.

Tapping Points:

TH = Top of Head

EB = Eye Brow

SE = Side of the Eye

UE = Under the Eye

UN = Under the Nose

Ch = Chin

CB = Collar Bone

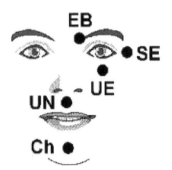

UA = Under the Arm

WR = Wrists

Now that you understand how to perform the tapping you will then need to know what to say while you are tapping.The traditional EFT phrases use the following setup:

"Even though I have this _____,I deeply and completely accept myself." You can also say "I deeply and completely love and accept myself."

The blank space above is filled in with a brief description of the emotion or problem you want to address. Before you start, rate your sensitivity to the issue on a scale of 1 - 10. Rate it yet again after you tap for a few rounds. You will often find your sensitivity levels dropping.

Example Using EFT Phrasing to Unblock Creativity

There really is no limit to the types of issues you can confront with EFT. The examples below are some that can help you release your natural creativity. Just repeat these while tapping all of the points.

"Even though I have this fear of expressing myself creatively, I deeply and completely accept myself."

You could also say:

"Even though I have this creativity block, I deeply and completely accept myself."

"Even though I am not sure if I am creative, I deeply and completely accept myself."

It really doesn't matter whether you believe the affirmations or not... just say them. Of course, it is much better to say the statements with feeling and emphasis, but saying it any way you want to say it will be fine.

To add to the effectiveness of the affirmations, state them out loud while you are tapping. As you are doing this, start concentrating on your issue. If you have a specific problem you are trying to solve, you can fine-tune the statements however you like.

Tuning in is a very simple process. You merely think about the problem while applying the tapping. That's it... at least in theory.

After you complete one or two rounds of tapping with the negative statement, you can then switch to a positive one. As you tap, repeat a statement like this:

"I am confident that my natural creativity is now being released and I deeply and completely accept myself".

Other statements might include things like this:

"The more I let go, the more my creativity shines through."

"I am a highly creative person, and this helps me in every area of life."

"The more I relax, the more intuitive and creative I am."

"I love being creative."

"My creativity helps me in every area of life from my relationships to my job."

In a nutshell, that's really all there is. Try tapping the next time you feel blocked or stumped on a problem, and you might be surprised at what comes rushing out!

Part II - Combining the Creative Mind with the Law of Attraction

Chapter Six: Using Your Creative Mind to Solve Life's Problems

"All creativity starts in the mind with a single solitary thought. It is your choice what you do with it." Leslie Riopel

The imagination was referred to as the "workshop of the mind" in Napoleon Hill's famous book, Think and Grow Rich. Many of us don't use this tool enough in our daily lives, but the reality is that it can help you picture your goals much more clearly.

When you use your imagination, you are tapping into your ability to daydream, which also helps you access the subconscious mind where changes are more easily made.

It pays to think like a child when it comes to using your imagination, because everything in life starts with a single thought. According to Napoleon Hill, there are two kinds of imagination, synthetic and creative. The synthetic imagination is where you rearrange old concepts, ideas or plans, so it's not as powerful as the creative imagination. When it comes to manifesting something with the Law of Attraction, nothing is more powerful than your own unique creative imagination.

Your creative imagination is limitless and infinite. Using the creative imagination you have access to your sixth sense, which is your gateway to your intuition and source of infinite knowledge.

People have been using tools like creative visualization and meditation for thousands of years and there are many schools of thought as to the history of it. Some scholars state that meditation can be traced back to the ancient practice of staring into the flames of a flickering fire.

Meditation is one of the oldest forms of spiritual, mental and health and wellness practices in existence and there is really no telling exactly how far back it goes.

There are so many benefits to visualization and meditation it is hard to list them all. Meditation helps you release stress and anxiety and it calms and relaxes the mind. Meditation can lower stress hormones, lower blood pressure and even help those with sleep disorders. Doing some kind of daily meditation, no matter if you meditate or visualize, is a wonderful way to start the day because it helps you ground and center yourself. Meditation and creative visualization is also a great way to help you tap into your own innate creativity and problem solving ability.

Meditation helps evoke something called the Relaxation Response, which helps you in many ways. Meditation helps you gain clarity and focus because it helps you slow your breathing down and relax your muscles.

Meditation can even help you increase your motivation and productivity by helping you focus on those things that you want to draw to you.

There are many health benefits to meditation and you don't really need any special skills to do so. Life can be overwhelming at times and meditation can help you cope better with the daily stress and strain of life. Engaging in a daily meditative practice can be done in as little as 5-10 minutes a day.

Health Benefits of Meditation

- Increases blood flow and slows the heart rate
- Decreases muscle tension
- Helps in post-operative healing
- Enhances energy
- Helps relax the nervous system
- Helps with weight loss
- Great for lowering blood pressure
- Can help relieve headaches
- Helps boost self-confidence
- Helps you control your thoughts
- Can increase serotonin levels
- Can enhance creativity and imagination
- Can help develop your intuition
- Helps you solve complex problems better
- Can help you boost your attitude
- Provides peace of mind and greater happiness
- Can help you bring the body, mind and spirit into alignment
- Can help you learn to be present in the moment

- Releases endorphins-your brain's natural feel good chemical

Tapping into your creative confidence can help you manifest things using the Law of Attraction. By combining your Creative Thought Library with your dreams and goals, there is no limit to the many things you can create in your life. It all starts with a single thought - it's as simple as that. Let's look at how you can do this now in some of those key areas of life. In this book we will examine four key areas:

- **Attracting Wealth and ProsperityUsing Creative Thought**
- **Attracting Health and Wellness Using Creative Thought**
- **Attracting Loving and Supportive RelationshipsUsing Creative Thought**
- **Creative Problem Solving**

If you're ready, let's get started!

Chapter Seven: Attracting Wealth and Prosperity Using Creative Thought

Your creative thought library can help you do much more than just solve problems. It can also help you manifest wealth and prosperity using the Law of Attraction. Wealth is one of those universal needs.

The truth of the matter is that it really isn't the wealth we desire, it's the feeling that having wealth gives us. What we really want is that feeling of safety and security prosperity brings us. When you have enough money to comfortably pay your monthly bills and you have enough money to be able to save a little each and every month, your life will feel much more balanced as a result.

Having wealth and prosperity really allows you to experience that feeling of relief and peace that having plenty of money brings you. Using the idea of a single point of focus, using your creative thought library, you will be both stunned and amazed at what you begin attracting into your life using these tools.

The more you focus on that feeling wealth and prosperity gives you, the more you will draw into your life new opportunities that will help you get there. The more detailed you get, the better the process works. Before we can dive into the wealth and prosperity exercise, it's important to have a basic understanding of how your senses work, in conjunction with the Law of Attraction.

NLP Sub-Modalities

When you use a tool like creative thought, you are using your five senses within your imagination. The more you can tune into your thoughts and ideas with your five senses, the more real your ideas become. This process is called neuro-linguistic programming.

Playing with your senses within the realm of visualization can work miracles and the techniques are endless. Visually you can brighten an image or make it larger to heighten its impact. When you use your imagination, colors have a big impact. The more you can see, sense and feel colors and textures, the more your mind accepts the images as real.

The concept of color works both ways - when you brighten the colors, you draw images too you, if you want to lesson something's impact you can turn the images black and white.

This also works wonders in the auditory mode because you can change the sound of something to change its impact as well. Kinesthetically you can feel an emotion or actually touch a soft fabric to soften the impact of something.

When doing these exercises, play around within these modes. Make the colors brighter or softer. Make the sounds louder or quieter. Turn the scene into a black and white scene or change the colors all together. The more you play with these different factors, the more you will improve your technique. The same goes for smells and tastes, when you are walking through a kitchen for example you can imagine what the room smells like or even taste foods sitting on the counter.

Visual Sub-Modality Brightness, color, shape, contrast, focus, movement, speed, three dimensional versus flat, transparency, density, orientation etc.

Auditory Sub-Modality: Pitch, tempo, rhythm, timbre, clarity, location, distance, loud or quiet etc.

Kinesthetic or Touch Sub-Modality: Pressure, texture, temperature, intensity, vibration, soft or hard, smooth or rough etc.

Olfactory or Gustatory Sub-Modality: Fading in and out ofsmells or tastes,odors, pungent or sweet smelling etc.

There are really only four basic steps when it comes to the Law of Attraction.

1.   Identify Your Desire
2.   Give Your Desire Attention
3.   Allow and Receive
4.   Take Action or Take Small Steps Towards Your Goals

The more you use your creativity muscle, the more you will develop it. The best way to use these tools are to take a few minutes out of every day and focus on that which you want to draw to you. It doesn't take a lot of time to do these exercises; the most important point of all is to do them consistently with a solid intention.

Using your creative thought library is as easy as taking these four simple steps. Identify, Give Attention To, Receive and Allow and Take Action. In this exercise, we are assuming you have already identified that you wish to work on wealth and prosperity, which means we can skip directly to the second step, which is giving your desire attention.

Begin by choosing a spot that is private and relaxing. Make sure you won't be disturbed. Give yourself at least 15 minutes to focus when doing this. You can start by doing some deep breathing or by sitting quietly and taking a few minutes to calm and relax yourself. Another option is to listen to some environmental sounds like the sound of waves or light rain. Environmental sounds work amazingly well for focus and concentration.

You can also begin by closing your eyes and simply observing your breathing, watching your breath as it goes in an out of your body. When thoughts come to you, simply acknowledge them and then dismiss them, do not judge them or get caught up in them. This practice is all about observing the thoughts for exactly what they are: thoughts. Thoughts do not define you or control you, they simply are. By observing in a detached way, you can disassociate from your thoughts and learn how to relax and let go of cares and concerns.

Get comfortable in your chosen spot, keeping your back straight. You can sit in a lotus position if you prefer or simply sit in a chair. Start to focus on your breath. Breathe slowly, allowing yourself to relax. Take a deep breath, and when you exhale, breathe out slowly. Feel the breath flowing out through your chest and swirling out around you, filling your energetic space with life energy. Take another deep breath and feel the relaxing energy.

Continue to relax and breathe... exhaling slowly....feel yourself sinking deeper and deeper into this feeling of relaxation. As you take in another deep

breath then slowly exhale, feel yourself
sinking into a feeling of peace.

Begin to call light to yourself, and
imagine with each inhale of your breath,
you are drawing in a beautiful white light,
and as you slowly exhale, that light is
spreading and vibrating throughout your
whole body. Allow yourself to bathe in
this healing light, and feel the peace and
the calm.

Now take yourself in your mind to
your unique creative thought library.
Spend a few minutes just enjoying the
environment all around you. Breathe in
your surroundings and notice where you
are. You may choose the same place every
time you do this, or you can choose
somewhere different and unique.

Now go inside....and look around,
notice what kinds of things you have in
this place. Start creating an environment
or room that fosters your creativity. Fill
the room with creative tools like
whiteboards and markers, easel pads,
comfortable chairs, paint brushes, any
books you may need, a computer, writing
surfaces, anything you can think of.

Now add anything else you think you need like a large viewing screen or theatre in the round; a beautiful garden with water or pools, a terrace or deck, or even a magical doorway that leads to other places in this library.

Think of this place like your own personal holographic structure - it becomes more real and more vivid each time you visit it. You will eventually get to the point where you can enter this daydreaming mode in a matter of minutes, every time you close your eyes and allow your mind to wander. This place is a very powerful place for healing, problem solving, future planning and even manifesting.

Take some time to enjoy being in this very creative space. Now, focus on your issue. Start to form an image in your mind of what wealth and abundance means for you. You can use your creative space and start filling it in with pictures and images of what wealth and prosperity mean for you.

You can draw or pretend you are using pictures from a magazine. Start putting up images all around the room, filling up every wall. You can use the whiteboard to write down what wealth means for you.

You might write for example:

- Feeling of safety and security
- Enough money to comfortably live
- A nice amount of disposable income
- Enough money to drive a new car
- Enough money to live in my dream home
- Enough money to travel and take lavish vacations, etc.

Write down anything you can think of. Now cover the walls with images of things that are important to you, as it pertains to wealth and prosperity. You might put up pictures of a beautiful home, a new car, exotic travel destinations, beautiful fabrics or material possessions, whatever you like. Take some time to really visualize these things. See yourself going around the room looking at these things. Immerse yourself in the idea of wealth and prosperity.

Now, ask yourself a series of questions.

- Exactly how much money do you see yourself making every month?
- How do you feel now that you have this money?
- How do you use your newfound wealth to make the world a better place?
- What do you do for a living or what is your passion?
- What kind of car do you drive?
- What kind of house/apartment/condo do you live in?
- What does the outside of your residence look like?
- What part of the country is it in?
- What does the inside look like?
- How do you spend your time?

Now take yourself into your new residence.....and really be there in your mind. Walk through the front door, and go room to room. See the colors, and the fabrics and make them bright and vibrant. Notice the paint color and the floors and sit on the furniture. Go into the kitchen and take a bite of something, maybe an apple sitting on the counter. Look out the window, and notice what you see. Listen for the sounds of the air conditioning or the furnace running. Open the cabinets and notice what kind of dishes you have. Make yourself a cup of coffee and sit and enjoy your new surroundings.

Keep walking around the house, making the images bolder and brighter. Touch and feel the textures and lay down on the soft bed. Run your hands along the counter in the bathroom, and notice all those tiny little details. See yourself getting ready in the morning and notice your routine. Go through your ideal day or just spend 10-15 minutes here soaking in all of the details. Go outside and sit on the deck or patio, or sit in the woods.

Notice any unique features in the house, like a fancy security system or home entertainment system. If you have children or a life partner or husband or wife that you love, imagine they are here, and sit down and enjoy a meal with them. Make it as real as you can.

Immerse yourself in your surroundings by listening, tasting, touching, feeling and seeing. Go out to the garage and notice what kind of car you drive. Is your house light and airy or cozy and dark?

What kinds of toys do you have - maybe a golf cart or motor scooter? Now imagine how you manage your great wealth now, notice your bank balance by sitting down at your home computer. Make a call to your financial advisor and chat with them. Ask yourself what your goal is now that you have achieved this one? Think about what you still want to accomplish in life.

Practice expressing some gratitude now so you can allow and receive graciously - thank the universe or God or whoever you choose for blessing you with such abundance. Express your appreciation. Feel the emotion of happiness you feel, and take some time to really express your gratitude. Thank the universe for all of this. On a quantum level, you have really already received all of this, so this is quite real. Express gratitude for those simple things in life you already have like a warm home, a healthy body or even the ability to walk or breathe. Work your way up to expressing gratitude for wealth and abundance as if you already have this gift.

This is a free form process, and one what will change every time you do this. You don't need to be too formal with this, simply allow your mind to wander and focus in on 5-10 things daily that you feel grateful for. Repeat as often as you like throughout the day.

As you go about your day, start paying attention to those little synchronicities or things that start occurring, now that you shifted your focus to that of abundance. Most of all take action when things start to happen. Make a point to take small steps towards your goal each and every day.

Affirmations

Affirmations are a great way to change your subconscious thoughts - you can either do them as part of your creative thought library process or you can do them throughout the day anytime you want. Create 5-10 statements set in the present tense that reflect the way you would feel with great wealth and abundance. If you do these as part of the process above, you can change them as much as you want.

Wealth and Prosperity Sample Affirmations

- The world is a generous and giving place
- I have everything I need right now

- I am always in the right place at the right time
- I am grateful for everything I have and everything I am about to receive

- I have all the money I need to take care of everything
- Money flows to me with ease
- I enjoy all of the luxuries of the world
- My resources are abundant
- Money is attracted to me
- I express my unique creativity and I am successful in everything I do.

- I am grateful.
- I am lucky to have tapped into this well of abundance
- My life is magnificent and it supports me
- I have enough talent to make all the money I could ever want
- Money comes to me whenever I need it
- I happily tap into the flow of abundance
- Abundance shines down on me
- I love my life
- My thoughts create my world
- I create my life with every thought I think
- I think only prosperous thoughts now

Chapter Eight: Attracting Health and WellnessUsing Creative Thought

Just like before, begin by choosing a spot that is private and relaxing. Make sure you won't be disturbed. Give yourself at least 15 minutes to focus when doing this. You can start by doing some deep breathing or by sitting quietly and taking a few minutes to calm and relax yourself. Another option is to listen to some environmental sounds like the sound of waves or light rain. Environmental sounds work amazingly well for focus and concentration.

You can also begin by closing your eyes and simply observing your breathing, watching your breath as it goes in an out of your body. When thoughts come to you, simply acknowledge them and then dismiss them, do not judge them or get caught up in them. This practice is all about observing the thoughts for exactly what they are: thoughts. Thoughts do not define you or control you, they simply are. By observing in a detached

way, you can disassociate from your
thoughts and learn how to relax and let go
of cares and concerns.

Get comfortable in your chosen
spot, keeping your back straight. You can
sit in a lotus position if you prefer or
simply sit in a chair. Start to focus on your
breath. Breathe slowly, allowing yourself
to relax. Take a deep breath, and when
you exhale, breathe out slowly. Feel the
breath flowing out through your chest
and swirling out around you, filling your
energetic space with life energy. Take
another deep breath and feel the relaxing
energy.

Continue to relax and slowly
breathe in... and slowly exhale....feel
yourself sinking deeper and deeper
where you are, letting go of all
distractions and thoughts. As you take
another deep breath then slowly exhale,
feel yourself growing very peaceful and
centered.

Begin to call light to yourself, and
imagine with each inhale of your breath,
you are drawing in a beautiful white light,
and as you slowly exhale, that light is
spreading and vibrating throughout your

whole body. Allow yourself to bathe in this healing light, and feel the peace and the calm.

Now take yourself in your mind to your unique creative thought library. Spend a few minutes just enjoying the environment all around you. Breathe in your surroundings and notice where you are. You may choose the same place every time you do this, or you can choose somewhere different and unique.

Now go inside....and look around, notice what kinds of things you have in this place. Start creating an environment or room that fosters your creativity. Fill the room with creative tools like whiteboards and markers, easel pads, comfortable chairs, paint brushes, any books you may need, a computer, writing surfaces, anything you can think of.

Now add anything else you think you need like a large viewing screen or theatre in the round; a beautiful garden with water or pools, a terrace or deck, or even a magical doorway that leads to other places in this library.

Think of this place like your own personal holographic structure - it becomes more real and more vivid each time you visit it. You will eventually get to the point where you can enter this daydreaming mode in a matter of minutes, every time you close your eyes and allow your mind to wander. This place is a very powerful place for healing, problem solving, future planning and even manifesting.

Take some time to enjoy being in this very creative space. Now, focus on your issue. Start to form an image in your mind of what health and wellness means for you. You can use your creative space and start filling it in with pictures and images of what health and wellness mean for you. These might be photos of healthy people exercising or running or walking, or healthy foods or even the kinds of clothing you might wear if you were able to be any size you like. You might also enjoy using pictures of different kinds of exercise programs like yoga or Tai-Chi or see yourself walking a 5K. If you are concerned with disease, you could visualize yourself getting a clean bill of health from your doctor. Just think about what optimal health and wellness means for you personally.

You can draw or pretend you are using pictures from a magazine. Start putting up images all around the room, filling up every wall. You can use the whiteboard to write down what good health means for you.

You might write for example:

- Feeling of strong and vibrant health
- Ability to move and stretch my body
- Newfound confidence because of a healthy body
- Freedom to pursue my passions
- Freedom from pain
- More active lifestyle, etc.

Write down anything you can think of. Now cover the walls with images of things that are important to you, as it pertains to health and wellness. You can put up any photos that emulate good health from pictures of yourself smiling to pictures of people running and playing on the beach. Take some time to really visualize these things. See yourself going around the room looking at these things. Immerse yourself in the idea of health and wellness.

Now, ask yourself a series of questions.

- How does it feel to be so healthy?
- How is your life different because of your new state of health?
- What kind of freedoms do you have now?

- What kind of activities do you now enjoy?
- What do you do for fun?
- How has your diet changed?
- How do you shop for foods?
- How do you maintain this high level of health?
- What does it feel like to move and stretch your body?
- How does it feel to be free of pain or free of disease?
- How has your daily routine changed?
- Do you workout or walk on a regular basis now?
- Reflect on anything that has changed with this shift in thinking.

Now imagine you are walking on the beach. Stretch your arms and take in the fresh air. Notice how good you feel. Move your arms and legs and stretch your calves. Move your hands up and down your body, and notice how nice it feels to be in good shape and in good health. You feel good now that you have taken on this new healthy lifestyle.

Begin to breathe slowly, taking a deep breath....... in through your nose...

and out through your mouth. Take in another deep breath and slowly exhale. As you relax, say to yourself mentally, "Abundant health and wellness are my birthright."As thoughts come to you, acknowledge them, and let them float away. Continue to relax and slowly breathe in… and slowly exhale.

Continue to relax and breathe… exhaling slowly….feel yourself sinking deeper and deeper into this feeling of relaxation. As you take in another deep breath then slowly exhale, feel yourself sinking into a feeling of peace.

Begin to imagine a beautiful healing light entering your body through the top of the head. Allow the light to move throughout your whole body from the top of your head to the tips of your toes, encircling you in light and love. Allow yourself to bathe in this light as you repeat: "I am filled with the light of love, peace and joy."

Now imagine that you are about to go on an amazing journey to a beautiful island, an island of transformation. This island is going to lead you to a beautiful place of healing. As you arrive on this island, you begin walking along a peaceful serene beach - it is a warm sunny day. As you walk, you notice the sound of the waves hitting the shoreline – you feel the sun on your skin. In the background you hear the gentle, rhythmic sound of the breeze as it blows over the sand. Feel the sea air, and taste the saltiness as the air penetrates and cleanses your skin as it filters the impurities out of your body.

You decide to take a walk inland, and before you know it, you hear the sound of a nearby waterfall, off in the distance. You imagine the beauty and the peacefulness that water brings, and you decide to investigate further, so you can bathe in this waterfall and shed the parts of you that are no longer supporting your abundant health.

As you approach the waterfall, you feel the mist even before you arrive. The water is peaceful and serene and it is a beautiful color – blues mixed with greens – beautiful healing colors. You decide to dip your toes into the water and it feels lovely. You may want to immerse your entire body into the peaceful water, if so, slowly imagine yourself sinking into this healing pond. – as the soft gentle water rolls off your skin.

You then decide to swim over to the waterfall, and stand underneath, as you shed the remaining parts of you that are no longer needed. Allow the water to flow over your head and down your body. Now imagine the water is now a beautiful color, any color you like. Imagine this color pouring over your body, cleansing you in a beautiful shower of light and love. You feel amazing and invigorated. The colors pour down over your body washing and cleansing your body of any and all impurities and toxins. You stay for a while longer in this amazing place, and then step out of the water into a soft robe that is waiting there for you.

As you walk, you soon discover a beautiful mirror, as you stand in front of this mirror; a beautiful veil appears right before your eyes – it is a lovely and shimmering veil; you find it enchanting and comforting. The veil shows you everything about yourself that you feel is special and important. You see everything you value about yourself. You see the labels you choose to wear proudly. You see your passions and dreams here. You see yourself in vibrant good health – and it feels good. The healing waters have cleansed your soul.

Now acknowledge your body. Your body has intelligence – it has a heart – it can heal itself. Everything has a frequency and a vibration – and you can tune into this healing frequency anytime you desire.

Begin to express appreciation and give thanks to how your body serves you. Begin at your feet and move up. Give appreciation and honor your feet – tell your feet and your legs how much you appreciate their service. Scan the body and become aware – give thanks as you connect with the body – in appreciation for how it serves you.

Now move up to the abdomen and the hips…..then thank the stomach, the colon, the spinal column, the heart – thank all your organs and tissues. Thank your neck and your shoulders, thank the chin and face, the nose, the tongue the eyes and the scalp. Scan the body all the way up and down and take the time to thank each and every part of you.

Your body is sacred – it is the greatest sacred geometry that you will ever see. It is a work of art expressed through your personality.

Notice how you feel - strong, and intelligent and powerful. You are vital and sacred. Allow yourself to fully honor and respect your body as your sacred temple. You have been gifted this body for a lifetime – and it is a work of art expressed as flesh and bone; a vehicle worthy allowing you to manifest and express perfect health.

Take a moment to just give thanks and to honor the temple that is the body.

Now express your intention to embrace wellness, wholeness, health and well being. You are so deserving – so honorable. It's OK tofeel good and to be healthy. It's OK to be strong – to have a high degree of vitality.

Feel how good it feels to let go of any thought patterns that may have blocked your healing in the past. See yourself loving your body – just as it is. Feel gratitude for every organ – give permission to be whole – to be healthy – to glow from within.

Pause…..

It feels so good to feel good again. You are enjoying these relaxing pleasant feelings so much. You have trained your mind to focus in on these good feelings and as a result, your mind rewards you by intensifying these feelings of comfort. The more you relax the better you feel - and the better you feel - the more you relax.

You know that everything you are or everything you will ever be is the result of those choices and decisions you make. You now know that being healthy is a matter of choice, and you are choosing good health. When you choose healthy lifestyle habits you find it is quite easy to stay healthy.

Now that you have developed these healthy lifestyle habits, you now look at food as fuel……….you now realize that just like an engine that runs more efficiently with the proper fuel, so does your body. You like looking and feeling healthy, and even find yourself craving healthy foods.

Practice expressing some gratitude now so you can allow and receive graciously - thank the universe or God or whoever you choose for blessing you with such good health. Express your appreciation. Feel the emotion of happiness you feel, and take some time to really express your gratitude. Thank the universe for all of this. On a quantum level, you have really already received all of this, so this is quite real. Express gratitude for those simple things in life you already have like a warm home, a healthy body or even the ability to walk or breathe. Work your way up to expressing gratitude for this gift of good health as if you already have this gift.

This is a free form process, and one what will change every time you do this. You don't need to be too formal with this, simply allow your mind to wander and focus in on 5-10 things daily that you feel grateful for. Repeat as often as you like throughout the day.

As you go about your day, start paying attention to those little synchronicities or things that start occurring, now that you shifted your focus to that of health and wellness. Most of all take action when things start to happen. Make a point to take small steps towards your goal each and every day.

Affirmations

Affirmations are a great way to change your subconscious thoughts - you can either do them as part of your creative thought library process or you can do them throughout the day anytime you want. Create 5-10 statements set in the present tense that reflect the way you would feel with optimal health and wellness. If you do these as part of the process above, you can change them as much as you want.

Health and Wellness Sample Affirmations

- I feel happy & healthy
- I breathe easily & deeply without effort
- My body now purges itself of anything that does not support my perfect health
- I have been blessed with a tremendously powerful immune system
- I grow stronger each & every day

- My perfect health is my true gift
- I now celebrate my divine health
- My body transitions easily to this new found freedom
- Every cell in my body feels alive
- My immune system now works perfectly and eliminates any abnormality or irregularity that may have existed in my body
- My body is a precious gift
- My body is an instrument, rather than an ornament
- I am happy with my body just like it is
- I am thankful for all my body does for me
- I can strive to improve my body, but be happy with it right now
- People love me for who I am on the inside
- I am unique, important and special
- I smile every day because I am worth it.

Chapter Nine: Attracting Loving and Supportive Relationships Using Creative Thought

Just like before, begin by choosing a spot that is private and relaxing. Make sure you won't be disturbed. Give yourself at least 15 minutes to focus when doing this. You can start by doing some deep breathing or by sitting quietly and taking a few minutes to calm and relax yourself. Another option is to listen to some environmental sounds like the sound of waves or light rain. Environmental sounds work amazingly well for focus and concentration.

You can also begin by closing your eyes and simply observing your breathing, watching your breath as it goes in an out of your body. When thoughts come to you, simply acknowledge them and then dismiss them, do not judge them or get caught up in them. This practice is all about observing the thoughts for exactly what they are: thoughts. Thoughts do not define you or control you, they simply are. By observing in a detached way, you can disassociate from your thoughts and learn how to relax and let go of cares and concerns.

Get comfortable in your chosen spot, keeping your back straight. You can sit in a lotus position if you prefer or simply sit in a chair. Start to focus on your breath. Breathe slowly, allowing yourself to relax. Take a deep breath, and when you exhale, breathe out slowly. Feel the breath flowing out through your chest and swirling out around you, filling your energetic space with life energy. Take another deep breath and feel the relaxing energy.

Continue to relax and breathe... exhaling slowly....feel yourself sinking deeper and deeper into this feeling of relaxation. As you take in another deep breath then slowly exhale, feel yourself sinking into a feeling of peace.

Begin to call light to yourself, and imagine with each inhale of your breath, you are drawing in a beautiful white light, and as you slowly exhale, that light is spreading and vibrating throughout your whole body. Allow yourself to bathe in this healing light, and feel the peace and the calm.

Now take yourself in your mind to your unique creative thought library. Spend a few minutes just enjoying the environment all around you. Breathe in your surroundings and notice where you are. You may choose the same place every time you do this, or you can choose somewhere different and unique.

Now go inside....and look around, notice what kinds of things you have in this place. Start creating an environment or room that fosters your creativity. Fill the room with creative tools like whiteboards and markers, easel pads, comfortable chairs, paint brushes, any books you may need, a computer, writing surfaces, anything you can think of.

Now add anything else you think you need like a large viewing screen or theatre in the round; a beautiful garden with water or pools, a terrace or deck, or even a magical doorway that leads to other places in this library.

Think of this place like your own personal holographic structure - it becomes more real and more vivid each time you visit it. You will eventually get to the point where you can enter this daydreaming mode in a matter of minutes, every time you close your eyes and allow your mind to wander. This place is a very powerful place for healing, problem solving, future planning and even manifesting.

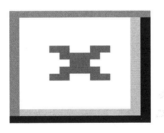

Take some time to enjoy being in this very creative space. Now, focus on your issue. Start to form an image in your mind of what your ideal relationship looks like and feels like. You can use your creative space and start filling it in with pictures and images of what love and intimacy mean for you. These might be photos of people walking hand in hand, people embracing or hugging or anything else.

You can draw or pretend you are using pictures from a magazine. Start putting up images all around the room, filling up every wall. You can use the whiteboard to write down some statements that reflect how you feel with a healthy loving relationship.

You might write for example:

- A feeling of deep intimacy and connection
- A feeling of love and acceptance
- Feeling of happiness and personal fulfillment
- Deep levels of respect and honesty
- Emotional freedom, etc.

Write down anything you can think of. Now cover the walls with images of things that are important to you, as it pertains to love and relationships. See yourself going around the room looking at these things. Immerse yourself in the idea of a healthy loving and supportive relationship.

Now, ask yourself a series of questions.

- What does love mean for you?
- What kind of relationship do you envision?
- What kinds of qualities are you looking for in a partner?Try and focus on personality characteristics rather than physical appearance. For example, you might want someone who is loving and caring, compassionate, respectful, understanding, strong, physically active etc.
- Do you see yourself single or married in this ideal relationship?
- If you are married, and desire a stronger relationship, focus on what originally drew you together.
- What kinds of things do you and your partner enjoy doing?
- How does it feel having a strong relationship to rely on?
- Where do you go on date night?
- How do you socialize?
- How do you show affection? Hugging, lightly touching? Holding hands?

- What does being intimate and affectionate feel like for you? (Focus more on the intimate connection as opposed to the sexual connection.)
- How do you resolve differences?
- How do you communicate?
- How do you handle money and finances?
- What do you do for fun?
- What do each of you do career wise?

In order to manifest love and be involved in a loving and healthy relationship you first have to love yourself. You have to shift your energy to one of love. Self-love is the start of all healthy relationships.

Begin by breathing in and imagine you are surrounded by the energy of love. Start by imagining a beautiful green or pink energy flowing out of your heart. Your body has seven powerful energy centers - these energy centers are called chakras. The heart chakra is the chakra of love.

See this energy surrounding you in a cocoon of love. Love can heal all wounds.

Allow yourself to bathe in this powerful energy, the energy of love. This is a powerful exercise whether or not you are actively seeking love or if you are merely working on self-love.

Now imagine what love looks like and what it feels like for you. The feeling of love is like a warm, comforting feeling. The energy of love feels safe and protected. Think about how you view love now. Think about those ways you love yourself and the way you show love to others. Love is very healing, so let go of any negative feelings you have as it pertains to love, whether it is jealousy, anger or anything else.

Now think about your place in the world as it pertains to love and affection? Are you happy and content? Do you feel love and express love to others? If not, why?

If you are happy and content with love, use this time to revel in those powerful emotions. There is always room to improve in love, because love is an endless emotionand an untapped resource.

If you are searching for love, use this time to shift your energy into the energy of love. Take some time to appreciate yourself for the beautiful person you are.

Feel this sense of love growing and nurturing you. Take some time to contemplate the emotion of love. Just keep envisioning that beautiful shade of green flowing out from your heart area. The power of love is always growing and always expanding.

Now ask yourself now how much you really love yourself? You are a divine spirit because you are love. Think about those qualities you seek in an ideal relationship? If you are already in a loving relationship, think about those ways that you could express your love more kindly and more openly. Relationships always need nurturing.

Now ask yourself if you are a good receiver of love? If not, ask yourself what you could do to change that.

Express some gratitude by loving those things and people you already have....like friends and family. Embrace yourself and your life flaws and all. Your eccentricities make you unique and special.

Ask yourself how you need to be in order to attract the right kind of person into your life or what kind of person you need to be to enjoy your current relationship more?

Now visualize yourself walking in a beautiful garden. Hear the sounds of the birds and smell the aroma of the flowers. Walk for a while and just enjoy the day, you might even notice water in a nearby stream.

Usethis time to simply enjoy some quiet time and to surround yourself with the energy of love. Now as you walk, imagine seeing a wooden bench. Sit down on the bench and reflect on your life, in terms of love. If you have a desire to heal a damaged relationship, imagine that the person you need to talk to is sitting next to you. Say what you need to say, but say it with great empathy and love and affection.

If you have a desire to attract someone new, imagine someone walking up to you, asking you if they can sit down. What kind of person do you imagine? Are they kind and compassionate? Open and loving? Tall or short? Whatever qualities you desire, think about them now.

This may be someone new, someone you have never met, or someone familiar and comfortable, you decide. You may sit with anyone or anything you like, this is your special time. A time to heal and a time to love.

Sit with this person for a while and just enjoy their company. Express love to them, even if it is only through a kind word or a hug. Imagine your heart is radiating out a lovely energy, the energy of love.

The energy of love has the power to transform your life. Now see yourself walking hand in hand with this person. Just walk and talk for as long as you like. Make the experience real. Feel the warmth and affection and appreciation.

This is NOT about sex, but rather about the emotional connection.

Allow this energy to work its magic in the coming days and the coming weeks. Allow love to heal and transform your life, in whatever way it needs to.

Practice expressing some gratitude now so you can allow and receive graciously - thank the universe or God or whoever you choose for blessing you with love. Think of all those people who are already in your life, like your family, your friends, even your pets or co-workers.

Express your appreciation. Feel the emotion of loveand affection, and take some time to really express your gratitude. Thank the universe for all of this. On a quantum level, you have really already received all of this, so this is quite real. Express gratitude for those simple things in life you already have like loving friends and family or even your ability to walk or breathe. Work your way up to expressing gratitude for this gift of love as if you already have this gift.

This is a free form process, and one what will change every time you do this. You don't need to be too formal with this, simply allow your mind to wander and focus in on 5-10 things daily that you feel grateful for. Repeat as often as you like throughout the day.

As you go about your day, start paying attention to those little synchronicities or things that start occurring, now that you shifted your focus to that of love and appreciation. Most of all take action when things start to happen. Make a point to take small steps towards your goal each and every day.

Affirmations

Affirmations are a great way to change your subconscious thoughts - you can either do them as part of your creative thought library process or you can do them throughout the day anytime you want. Create 5-10 statements set in the present tense that reflect the way you would feel in a loving and supportive relationship. If you do these as part of the process above, you can change them as much as you want.

Loving and Supportive
Relationships Sample Affirmations

- I am attractive and worthy of love
- I love myself unconditionally
- People enjoy spending time with me
- People are attracted to my energy
- I have a magnetic personality
- I have many friends whom I enjoy spending time with
- I am worthy of great love
- I am worthy to receive love because I offer love freely
- I no longer let relationships take my life over, because I am happy with myself
- I have many friends whom I enjoy spending time with
- I don't need someone to complete me
- I enjoy spending time with myself
- I enjoy keeping myself fit and healthy, so I am always confident
- I am well-aware that I have much to offer
- I seek out people that complement me
- I no longer try to fix people
- I am filled with love and hope

- My relationships are amazing
- My relationships are satisfying and lovely
- I have a great sense of confidence now, and it shows
- My radiance attracts people

Chapter Ten: Creative Problem Solving

"Creativity is a drug I cannot live without" – Cecil B. DeMille

This little exercise is a fun one to do right before you go to bed. If you have a problem that is weighing on your mind, the best way to solve it is to let your subconscious mind go to work on it. When you are tired or sleepy, your mind is in that twilight state. You can actually program your mind to solve problems while you sleep. Try this the next time you have a problem you can't seem to solve. Just repeat this right before falling asleep stating your problem where the blank lines are.

I now instruct my subconscious mind to solve a problem. My mind is now easily able to reveal answers to me and form original and unique ways for me to solve the problem. Problems are merely opportunities for growth, and every problem has a solution and that solution or solutions will be revealed to me shortly. I now tap into the unlimited resources that my mind has, because the answers are within me. I expectantly await creative answers to form in my mind and float up to the surface, where they become instantly available. I instruct my mind now to begin formulating an answer or solution to my problem of _____, and while I sleep the solution will become available to me upon awakening, and I will recall every detail.

I imagine now that as I go to sleep tonight, my subconscious mind will work on my problem of _____, bringing me a wonderfully creative solution in the morning. If I do not sense the answer upon awakening, I rest easily knowing the solution will simply come to me, at some point during the day. I take a moment now to envision my problem, kindly asking my subconscious to reveal the answer to me now, if it has already been formulated, resting easily if nothing comes to mind, knowing that the answer will be revealed in the morning.

Pause for a moment.

These suggestions, and this issue are now firmly embedded into my subconscious mind, and my mind will now formulate the answer as I sleep. As I count from one to five, I will emerge from this relaxed state, feeling refreshed and relaxed, and ready for a good nights sleep. Number one, beginning to emerge. Number two, becoming aware of my surroundings. Number three, looking forward to positive results from this hypnosis session. Number four, feeling amazing and optimistic. Number five, fully emerged and ready for a restful nights sleep.

Conclusion

"Don't think. Thinking is the enemy of creativity. It's self-conscious, and anything self-conscious is lousy. You can't try to do things. You simply must do things" – Ray Bradbury

This book explored many areas as it pertains to creative confidence. You can use your mind and your creativity to attract anything you want, need or desire. When you take steps to expand your creativity, your life will open up in ways you might never imagine.

We can all use a little more creativity, because creativity and innovation are what allow us to learn and change and grow.The idea of creative confidence is really all about realizing the fact that each of us is gifted with a virtually unlimited potential for learning and creativity.The fact of the matter is that every single one of us is born as a genius. It's only when we are told what to do and how to do it that we begin to lose this natural creativity.

Using your imagination, you can create powerful visualizations that reflect the life you want to be living. I hope you enjoyed learning more about the process of creativity and I hope you enjoyeddoing these exercises. In the end, your creativity will make the world a better place.

If you would like to learn more about using meditation and visualization please check out my website or YouTube channel for links to future videos and exercises you can do at home. I hope you enjoyed this journey as much as I have!

I bid you peace.

Reference:

http://www.nature.com/scitable/blog/brain-metrics/are_there_really_as_many

http://www.ncbi.nlm.nih.gov/pubmed/19226510

http://patrickdriessen.blogspot.com/2009/04/think-out-of-box.html

http://answers.google.com/answers/threadview?id=747226

http://www.huffingtonpost.com/2012/10/20/daydreaming-creativity-mind-wandering_n_1981546.html

http://pasadenavilla.com/2014/03/14/daydreaming-and-mental-health/

18125673R00071

Made in the USA
Middletown, DE
21 February 2015